heart
-to-
heart,

♡

soul
-to-
soul

SAKURA HANAMI

# heart -to- heart, ♡ soul -to- soul

LOVE POEMS FOR YOU AND ME

Copyright @ 2024 by Sakura Hanami
All Rights Reserved.

No part of this book may be reproduced, distributed, transmitted or amended in any form or by any means, including photocopying, recording, or other electronic or mechanical methods, without prior written permission of the publisher, except in the case of brief quotations embodied in reviews and specific other noncommercial uses permitted by copyright law. No graphics or images from this book may be copied or retransmitted without the publisher's express written permission.

Hardcover ISBN: 978-1-0688444-2-3
Paperback ISBN: 978-1-0688444-3-0
Ebook ISBN: 978-1-0688444-4-7

To my soulmate and the journey to live
from the heart. Cheers to loving and
being loved from our wholeness.

Dear Soul,

I know you love love.

That's why you are here.

Perfectly as you are.

I desire that you dream big, beautiful dreams that make your heart swell with joy.

May these poems touch your heart and inspire you to love and expand from the deepest part of your soul.

Let your life unfold as beautifully as you were created.

I am rooting for you, my friend.

Let the adventure begin...

Love,

Sakura

# TABLE OF CONTENTS

## COMING HOME

With you,
I am challenged
to be my best;
I am urged
to look deeper within;
I am asked
to show the parts that hurt;
I am pushed
to confront my comfort zone;
I am supported
to let go;
I am appreciated
for the way I am;
I am loved
for who I am.
Thank you for bringing me
closer to home
and being the companion
to my soul.

# WHEN YOU KNOW

I finally feel I have met you
because you resonate with the love
that powerfully resides in me.
You are home to me because
I feel a coziness in my soul.
I know you are the one
I came to rendezvous with
in this world.
The others were to be released.
My soul was waiting for me
to trust myself again.
My light glows brighter
and more prominent with you.
I took a journey through
a million years,
and here I am
to experience this gift opening with you—
a chance to witness my essence
and presence with yours.
I am beyond blessed;
thank you for meeting me here.
My trust was beyond
what my eyes could see,
I was faithing the facts,

and I'm glad I did.
I know we are meant to be.

# FALLING FOR YOU

Since I was thirteen years old
I made wishes on shooting stars
to one day meet you.
I wondered if you were watching
the same stars
and desiring the same.
I spoke into the clear sky
and maybe you heard me
on a message carried on a blazing star.
I have been on quite the adventure
since that time,
meeting souls who never quite fit
and sometimes, I wanted to quit.
As I look up at the sky so lit,
I am reminded that love is everywhere—
and in time,
our wishes will collide
with each other
showering us with fireworks
as we fall for each other.

# BEING MYSELF

When I am alone
and in my presence,
I feel safe,
I feel free,
I feel wholesomely me.
When I am with you
and in your presence,
I feel safe,
I feel free,
and I feel wholesomely me.
This is why I enjoy you so much—
I can be alone and be myself
and I can be with you and be myself.
You see me and I see you.
Everything is perfect,
everything is right—
this is the truth.

# IN MY HEART

I look at you—
I love the way you look at me.
I love the way you smile
with your boyish charm,
I love the smell of you after you shave,
and the way your face caresses my cheek.
I love the notes you write for me—
your penmanship extending
from your heart.
I love how you make me laugh
when you teach me to fish and play tennis.
I love the gentle and patient way
you listen to my stories.
I love how you write to me,
speaking love to my soul.
I love the way you have passion
for everything you do,
and I love the way you
play music for me—
you inspire my soul with every note.
I love that you let me warm my cold feet
on your calves
and you fancy all my writing
and my art.

sakura hanami

I love that I came here to share this life
with you.

## ADVENTURES

Life as a single person—
was a necessary time to embrace myself
and realize true enjoyment
must be found within.
This fear we have
believing we are alone—
we are never alone,
I am not alone.
Angels and divine protection surround me,
when I take the time to align myself
to truth, to love, and to light,
my path is clear,
and everything flows.
I have the sweetest interactions
with the kindest of souls.
I was never alone,
I am not alone,
I am whole.
The adventure of a single person is fun,
the adventure of sharing my life is fun, too.
Whether in a partnership or not,
coming back to my wholeness
allows my future to burst
with more excitement.

Here I am,
soaking it all in
and now I understand my time alone
was for me to love me
so I can love you.

# FREE TO LOVE

Healing the anxiety,
healing the fears,
healing the wounds,
healing the pains,
left me an open vessel
for my soul to be free,
I have a clear path to you—
beyond the world,
beyond the program.
This is my soul ready to receive.

sakura hanami

## HARMONY

I am Yin,
you are Yang.
You are a complement
to everything I am.
We change together;
like the ocean kisses the sand.
I am the sky,
you are the mountain,
I am the moon,
you are the sun,
I am salt,
you are pepper,
I am sweet,
you are spice,
I am your woman,
you are my man.
Together, we have a balance
and life is a harmonic dance.

# MUTUAL CREATION

When I imagined you—
I could smell the sandwiches on the plane,
I could hear the other people rustling
in their chairs,
I could see you putting my luggage
in the upper cabin,
I could taste your kiss,
I could feel your hand holding mine.
Everything I imagined was real,
and your love was infused in my soul.
This is how I recognized you.

## JUST RIGHT

There were times when I yearned
to meet you in this world—
it felt surreal that you were out there
and when we finally met,
it was the most natural experience
of my life.
Like a breeze on a sunny mountain hike,
like a sweat bead in the hot Asian sun,
like a watermelon blueberry bubble tea,
like a mango and pineapple fruit cup,
like melt-in-your-mouth sushi,
like the best-fitting sneakers,
and miso soup and rice.
What a delicious delight to appreciate
you into my life.

# BORN TO BE

I sensed you deep in my heart
before I met you.
You felt like someone I could grow
and expand with forever,
you would allow me to know myself
better than I have before,
you would help me to surrender
the last pieces of what I had to let go,
you opened the door to more divinity
than I could know on my own,
you embraced the entirety of who I am
to help me receive all I desired.
You lived in my heart
until you came alive in my world.

## ONCE IN A LIFETIME

Meeting you
feels like
catching a train that only comes
once in a thousand years,
eating a delicious gluten-free cupcake,
dancing on a rainbow,
love letters written on gold tablets,
all-you-can-eat gourmet sushi,
floating down a chocolate river
on a marshmallow life raft,
and so much more
words cannot express.

# HOLISM

Spiritually, you flew into my heart,
emotionally, you grew into my being,
mentally, you blew into my mind,
physically, you came through my
awareness.

## COLLIDE

I don't know the exact time or place,
where you and I will collide.
Who will find the other first?
I imagine it will be
love at first sight—
I feel you in my soul
so I'm sure to recognize you.
It will be an adventure to learn
what brought our souls together
and all the exciting things
we will uncover.
I feel excited life is opening my heart
and yours is opening, too.
We will be two ships meeting in the night,
with a lot to share,
a lot to give,
a lot of light,
and a lot to love.

# COMPLEMENT

Your soul is what calls me to you,
your heart is what draws me to you,
your safety is what allows me to open up
to you,
your friendship is what brings me to play
with you,
your being is what inspires me to you,
your character is what makes me sticky
to you,
your kindness is what puts me in sync
with you,
your honour is what makes me melt to you,
and it is because of all these things
that make you perfect for me.

## MISSION ACCOMPLISHED

I get to live in this lifetime
knowing I came here to find you
and experience heaven with you.
I appreciate all that you are—
at this moment,
in every moment.
I will leave here
knowing you knew
how much you were loved.

# MAGIC RECIPE

Women love love;
men love respect.
Love means respect for women;
respect means love for men.
In our souls,
we have both masculine
and feminine qualities.
We are all capable of love and respect—
our soul will seek balance in the other;
a little bit of this,
a little bit of that.
This is the magic recipe of oneness.
This is the magic recipe of relationship.

# OUT-OF-THIS-WORLD

My heart has been wounded
many times before.
I'm not sure if I was made
for a world like this.
Nonetheless, here I am.
I long for a supernatural love—
one that is out-of-this-world.
Perhaps I arrived
from a distant planet,
struggling to make a life
as a free spirit on Earth.
Come play with me?

# EASY TO LOVE

I believed in soulmates for as long
as I can remember—
with every failed relationship,
I forgot they existed.
My friend would tell me
you can't put a square peg in a round hole,
yet I still tried with much effort.
Call it honour or call it foolish.
It took time to embrace my uniqueness
and when I stopped accepting common
or making things fit
where they didn't belong,
I welcomed an uncommon love.
A love that would embrace my totality
and wrap me in a golden blanket.
I have been blessed in this life.
God didn't let me have the ones
I thought I wanted
but he was growing me into someone
who knew I deserved more.
Like a dream, it all happened—
angels brought me my true soulmate,
one who fits,
one who feels right,

sakura hanami

one who I don't have to be someone else,
one who meets my soul with its wholeness,
and just like that,
everything fits.

## ON FIRE FOR YOU

I wouldn't want to do this
with anyone else.
I trusted God would answer
my prayers.
Believe me,
it got quiet for a long time.
I held a spot in my heart
for you and kept it warm with love
so your heart knew where
to come home to.
I have left the light on for you
and I am so happy now
that we get to burn our fires together.

# PERFECT LOVE

I used to read a lot
of relationship books,
and when I met you,
I didn't need them anymore.
You understood me,
and I understood you.
I was myself,
and you were you.
There was no decoding necessary.
We came from an open book
and set the slate wide open.
We gave each other
unconditional love—
the love we each had
and we built the rest together.
This is what it's like
when you meet a soulmate.

# PERFECT CIRCLE

Wholeness is a beautiful thing—
wholeness of spirit,
wholeness of God,
wholeness of self-love,
wholeness is a precursor to soulmate love.
Wholeness gave me alignment
and brought me
to the full goodness of life.
When I could be whole,
I could receive the gifts of my heart
and naturally, the soulmate to my soul.

# BALANCE

Balance is a beautiful thing.
As a woman,
when I tune into the energy around me—
naturally, I feel at home in a supportive
and encouraging place.
As an energetic yin being—
I like cozy, soft and welcoming;
it lets my soul relax and feel safe.
I feel best with a strong man
who can let me come out and play,
knowing he will protect me.
It's not that I can't defend myself,
but it allows me
to be free-spirited and fun.
I don't want to carry the world alone;
I would instead tend to our love.

# HAPPY PRINTS

I am blessed
to have met soulmates in my life—
some I have known my entire life,
some I have said goodbye in my heart,
some I have met for a season,
some I have yet to meet.
Soulmates have a certain quality to them—
their heart gets joyous
about the same things that make me smile,
their heart gets sad about the same things
that make me cry,
their heart knows what to say to me
when I am falling apart,
their heart knows when to say
nothing at all,
their heart is so in tune with mine,
both made of the same heart essence.
Soulmates will touch me forever—
and leave happy feet in my heart,
and all I will remember
is the love we shared.
Soulmates enlighten our path
and remind us how
beautiful and sacred

it is to cross paths with another
who reflects our brightness
in the same way.

# ON CALL

No matter where you are,
I can speak to your soul
because it listens for me—
waiting for my food to cook,
drawing a bath,
waiting for my computer to start,
looking at the night sky,
waiting for my Uber ride,
listening to my favourite song,
waiting for my hair to dry,
meditating after a workout,
this is how I know your soul.
You are always with me,
in the best parts of my day,
in the mundane parts of my day,
in the peaceful parts of my day,
my heart is connected to yours.

# UNION

This is the wonder of life—
here I am,
there you are.
Our lives are interconnected
at this specific time on Earth.
I was led through a maze to be here;
you were led through a storm.
Together, we experience heaven
and light our way home—
this is the wonder of life.

# MEETING NEEDS

Men need to be admired,
appreciated,
accepted,
and acknowledged
for the greatness they behold.
Women need to be heard,
understood,
empathized with,
and treated with care
for the beauty they embody.
It seems simple,
but often, we are coming from
our own perspective.
When you know what someone needs,
you are more apt to give it.
Let's support each other
to be our best.
Ultimately,
it is a gift to share this life
with each other—
why wouldn't we want to do it
in the most potent way?

sakura hanami

# HUNKY MAN

The truth is—
I want your masculine energy in my life,
so I can relax into who I am.
If I'm honest with myself,
I'm juggling a part
I'm not very good at—
I've become sufficient at it.
I welcome you—
hunky man.
I welcome you into my life,
to be my man.
I am excited to lean on you,
and bring more joy into your life, too.
We will be the toppings
on a yummy sundae—
adding more electricity
to our tasty life.

# DOUBLE POWER

Choosing a partner from a soulful place
means choosing a reciprocity of authenticity
between two people—
choosing to be kind,
choosing to be vulnerable,
choosing to be honest,
choosing to be upfront,
choosing to speak to one another
respectfully,
choosing to clear up misunderstandings,
choosing to be there for each other,
choosing to share everything.
Choosing like this will feel good
for your soul.
This partnership is one of faith
for both people
trusting the other person—
will love you for the most authentic part
of you,
will protect your sacred bond
and not destroy it,
will help you to win and not compete,
will grow with you and not away from you.
This is where two people
can move mountains together.

sakura hanami

# BRIDGE

We all have needs,
sometimes unmet as children.
We will often seek partners
who help us meet those needs.
We desire intimate relationships
to bridge us to a healed place.
Without the inner work
to heal our wounds,
we often won't recognize
our wholeness and instead,
attract partners
that exacerbate our pain.
When we continue to grow,
surrender our past
and persist in the work,
God will bring us another soul
who mirrors our wholeness
to create a balance of yin and yang.
This is the beauty of a teammate.

# WHAT I ADMIRE

There are so many things
I admire about you.
You are a gentlemen.
You are also kind,
strong,
intelligent,
and consistently trying to grow.
I feel safer when you are around.
I sleep more soundly when you are near.
I know you will always try to protect me
from everything that concerns me.
I love that you lead me
from your loving
and respectful heart.
I appreciate all you do
and the thoughtfulness
behind your actions and words.
You have made me your family
and welcomed me
like I was always a part of you.
I admire and appreciate who you are.

# LOVE CANAL

Only with an open heart
can a person witness its counterpart.
The soul exists in the deep,
so another must meet it there.
Both have to jump through the love canal
often while embracing uncertainty.
Only when both people take a leap
can they discover the depth
of another's soul.

heart-to-heart, soul-to-soul

# CLEAR NUDGE

I knew you were the one
when you weren't like anyone
from my past.
We met when I followed my heart,
and you were true to yourself.
We both had survived an apocalypse.
In the rubble,
we found each other
guided by divine nudges on our path—
a light in the dark,
water after a drought,
sun peaking after the storm,
cold hands on a hot steering wheel,
a pearl in an oyster.
Everything led me to you.

# COLLABORATE

I love that we co-create our lives together.
You are my teammate and best friend.
You are the easiest person
I have ever been with,
because you care about me
in the same way I care about you.
Some may say we care more
about one another than we do ourselves.
I think it's because we know
that without each other,
this wouldn't be our rodeo.
I love that we create this loving space,
the way we want it.
We honour each other
and help each other,
because we know the health
of our relationship
depends on the health of the other.

# I'M PROUD OF YOU

Every day, I'm proud of you.
I'm proud of the way you care
for the people you love.
I'm proud you are passionate
about your purpose.
I'm proud you seem to have
superpowers when everyone else
has run out of fuel.
I'm proud you are my rock
when everything around me
is squishy and uncertain.
I'm proud you are the person
I can go to you
and be reassured that life will be okay.
I'm proud you are
everything God made you to be.

# CLOAKED IN GOLD

One day we will meet,
you will be ready for me
and I will be ready for you.
There will be magic in our energy fields—
a golden mist of heaven.
It will be like opening the best book—
filled with joy, laughter, love, and mystery.
We will enjoy each other,
and our souls will have a party.
We will know about the four horsemen,
yet we will know more about honour,
kindness, truth, and love.
This is the experience of knowledge
and heart work,
yet surrendering—
letting go and letting God.

# BOUNDLESS

What is love?
Love is that power
that takes over your body
and fills your spirit.
It is the mind disappearing,
and melting into an abyss.
It is endless,
limitless,
boundary-less,
expansive.
It is home
and knowing we are all connected.
It is beyond me
and everywhere—
love is what is.

# TEAMMATE

We are the winning team.
I couldn't have asked for a better partner.
We laugh and smile when
life gives us lemons or sunshine.
You step up when I need to sit down.
You climb higher when I need to melt
into the ground.
You bounce,
and I am bounced higher.
I am here for you always,
as you are here for me.
You provide things for me
I couldn't on my own.
You do everything from your heart,
and you only do it to see me smile.
We are the best team,
and I only want to play
this life with you.

## LIFE NAVIGATION

Sometimes I cry
because the world shows me things
I don't want to see.
But I will take all those things,
because it allows me to see
beautiful things like you.
I have been enlightened to it all.
I will appreciate
that I can see at all.
You weather these storms with me
and remind me,
I can close my eyes
and be in a world
we create together.
Together, we share Heaven on Earth,
because we make it part of our mission.
This is how I navigate the world—
with my co-pilot at my side.

sakura hanami

# HEART WISDOM

My father told me to keep my heart open
in a whisper to my soul.
It is a message
I hear often
and I know he is right.
In these challenging times,
it is easy to forget,
but then I remember,
when I lead from my heart,
the best of life
can meet me at this level.

heart-to-heart, soul-to-soul

# HEART TRUTH

When I listened to my intuition,
I knew in my heart it was you—
we could have the deep conversations,
you could lead me from your security,
you had sound intelligence,
you had deep wisdom from introspection,
you could connect
with your authentic emotions,
you could be present in discomfort.
Most of all,
it's your integrity
that calls my heart to you—
the invisible code of principles
that are present in who you are.

sakura hanami

# TREASURE

Two minds,
two hearts;
One love.
One soul.
You are the one who inspired
this poetry to exist.
I write these poems
because I know one day
you will read them.
Our souls are destined to meet
and what a treasure it will be.
I promise to love you
for the rest of my days
I am blessed
to be graced
with you.

## SPARKS

Meeting soulmates
has taught me how good life can be—
when you can be with someone
who sees you heart-to-heart
and adores you soul-to-soul.
Meeting soulmates
has made me excited to
uncover more of these people
who walk this earth.
I am bound to come across
my person soon.

# DIVINE CREATION

God places these desires,
big and small, into my heart.
When I finally understood
that God fulfills me,
every one of my desires
made an entrance into my life.
The soulmate I was searching for
fell into my awareness.
He is the gift from God who beats
in sync with my heart.
I can see forever in his eyes,
and the beauty of his soul
takes me on a whimsical journey with him.
His love for God allows him to honour me
in the way I deserve.
The past is gone, and my present
and future belong with him.
All I desire has come my way.
You are my best friend,
and my soul's love.
God created you for me.

## LIFE-GIVING

You raised me higher
and that was my first soul-knowing
that souls can give you life.
They can provide you with breath
when you can't breathe,
they can nourish you when you are empty,
they can shelter you
when you are in a storm,
they can give you fire when you are lost,
they can provide you with hydration
when you are parched,
and most of all,
they can give you things
you didn't know you needed,
until they greet your soul
and you are reminded of what a treasure
it is to be found.

## KING AND QUEEN

Deep in my soul
I need you.
My feminine grace
is soft and gentle,
my heart is a flower.
I need your protection,
your masculine safety
when the winds are too strong,
when my tears have no place to land,
when my beauty needs
a witness from your spirit,
when I smile in your presence,
when I am me in my receptivity,
when I need to be held,
when my petals need caressing,
when I need to whisper
into your kind heart
and be adored in your arms.
I need you to know me
and understand me,
to be my king.
I have felt your essence within me.
I know you, and I welcome your presence.

# YOU ARE MY MAN

In my world before you,
I had to do all the tough stuff
that came unnaturally to me.
I love that you can carry things so easily—
what takes me hours,
can quickly take you minutes.
I love it when you shovel the snow
and I dance and cheer
watching you work hard.
I love it when you maintain the cars,
and I can sing,
be safe, and free when I drive.
I love it when you work out
and care for your strong body
so our kids know about excellent health.
I love it when you plan
for our future,
and I can plan things for our home.
I love that you care for me
so I can do what comes naturally to me.
I love the man you are.

# DREAM COME TRUE

I have never met anyone like you.
You see all the parts of me
I desire to be seen.
You know all the parts of me
I desire to be known.
I feel witnessed by you.
And I feel at peace with you.
There is no part of me
I keep from you.
You have shown me,
my soul is safe with you.
I feel free with you.
This is what people dream of.
This is what I dreamed of.
This dream is ours.

## SET FREE

Being with you—
is as easy as breathing.
This is coming from a girl
who hasn't had anything easy.
I quickly saw you helped me relax
and openly receive.
I have had to guard my heart
with such fierceness in the past.
But with you,
everything is different.
Your generous heart
gives me room to be
and loves me more for my authenticity.
Thank you for holding me steady so
my heart can dance so freely.

# PLAYGROUND

I get to be vanilla,
and you get to be my chocolate.
I get to be saucy,
and you get to be dashing.
I get to be cute,
and you get to be charming.
I get to be pretty,
and you get to be handsome.
I get to be a dreamer,
and you get to be a visionary.
I love that you let me be who
I want to be,
and you play along with my silliness.
You are my playmate;
and what a blast it is
to create art with you.
You are my favourite place
to be everything I want to be.

# I SEE YOU

You have always been the one
who treated me with love.
You never let the sun go down
without telling me you care.
You speak the language
of my heart,
and it makes me melt.
You know when I need extra time
to be with myself
and when I need
to surrender in your arms.
You allow me to be who I am
and who I want to be—
and with you, it's the same.
You make my life better.
I choose you every moment
of my days.

# THE SOUL KNOWS

In picking a partner,
there is always a risk.
In a good fit,
there will be a knowing
that this person
is safe,
loving,
kind,
and good.
Not sometimes—
but especially when it is difficult,
inconvenient,
and when nothing makes sense.

# SOUL VISION

I will let my heart lead the way—
with the vision from my soul.
I will walk forward
because I know your heart
is leading you, too.
When two souls desire the same,
the divine will make a way.

# HECK YES

Every man who I had ever been with
had been a "no" in my heart.
And then another fellow
came into my life
and my heart said yes.
He broke my heart
so God told me
he will choose the next one.
And this time
I know my heart will
say, "heck yes".
God wants me on fire
for the right things.

# TEDDY BEAR

If I'm totally honest,
I love that you are strong.
I love your muscles
and effortless strength.
I love that you catch me staring at you.
I love that I feel small in your arms.
I love the way you easily catch me
when I do a running jump to greet you.
I love that you take up the whole couch,
and I get to climb on you.
I love that you give me a hard time,
but love my kisses and affection.
I love how you tease me
but would never dare hurt me.
I love that you know these things
and always receive me.
I love you because you are my big
teddy bear in this wild world.
Thank you for loving me
the way you do.

# FOREVER LOVE

I get to do this journey with you
and I am so humbly grateful.
It took me some time to find you,
but this is lovely.
It's like home-fried chicken,
baked yesterday
and I get to devour it today.
Everything tastes so much better—
more flavourful,
more spicy,
more chewy,
more scrumptious,
more delicious.
This is my favourite way—
appreciating all the details.
You are my home-fried chicken
who gets richer and deeper—
everything I love
greeting me day after day.

# RECEIVING YOU

In the airport of my heart,
I stay open—
to kind people,
to loving messages,
to the correct arrival.
Not everything will I accept.
My heart knows
the exciting adventures that await
when a heart is lit up for me.
I only want what's meant for me.
God labelled you "heaven sent"
and indeed, you are.

# COLLUSION

Our souls have already chosen each other.
I trust the power
that lives in us
to bring us together.
Today,
I am so happy and grateful
our souls have been colluding
this setup,
our entire lives.

# DESTINED

I was meant to be here,
at this moment in history—
this era,
this time
and this space.
You were meant to be here, too.
When my heart beats
next to yours,
I feel forever in this moment.
I am in awe
how everything led to this.

# WITNESS

I see the way you look at me
and the way you pay attention
to all the little things—
the stray hair on my face,
the gloss on my lips,
the excitement in my laughter,
the movement of my hands,
the caress of my fingers,
the bounce in my step,
the wiggle in my hips,
the squeeze in my hugs,
the story in my eyes,
the pain in my tears,
the inspiration in my breath,
the spirit in my being,
the love in my heart.
I love the way you see me.

# PROFOUND

This time,
it will happen quickly—
because I will let my soul choose.
The soul doesn't hum and haw.
It knows right from the get-go.
There will be signs and wonders
that can only be connected
looking backward.
This is how all great stories unfold.

# HOME

When I met you,
I felt something click deep in my soul.
Your eyes felt like home to me,
your touch felt soothing to my heart,
your voice danced within me,
your kindness recognized me,
your love held space for me.
God protected me from all the other boys
until that fateful day
your soul met mine.

# GOD MADE ME

When I am in your presence,
you respect me,
you care for me,
you are a gentleman,
you witness all the parts of me,
I desire to be treasured.
You are my man,
you have my heart,
you have my soul,
you have my presence.
I am entirely the woman
God made me to be.

# LIKE AND LOVE

I like the way you are,
I like the way you think,
I like the way you try,
I like the way you introspect,
I like the way you meet me,
I like the way you share with me.
I like the way you see into me
I like the way you love me
but most of all,
and I love who you are.

# LOVE FITS

I love the way your hands
feel in mine.
I love the way they hold my body.
I love the way your hands discover me.
I love the way your hands fit mine.
I love that no one has ever felt this way.

# CHOOSING YOU

You are my best friend.
You are my soul mate.
You are the man I admire and respect.
You are the man with whom
I share deep passion and trust.
You are the person I choose
for the rest of my life.

# SLICE OF HEAVEN

When two souls find each other
and bring out the best in each other—
Heaven on Earth.

# HOW WE KNEW

I knew you were the one.
My soul felt safe with you.
Your depth tickled my mind.
Your presence treasured my heart.
Your courage protected my presence.
My spirit was loved by your open heart.
My love was received and reciprocated.
Your story was the same,
and we were on the same page
in our book of love.
You knew I was the one.

heart-to-heart, soul-to-soul

# HOLISTIC LOVE

In your arms,
I feel safe physically,
I feel safe emotionally,
I feel safe mentally,
I feel safe spiritually;
you are my home on earth.

## SEASONS

I used to be sad
when partners left my life
but now I understand,
sometimes life moves people away,
so I can welcome
a soul who dances with mine—
in all the seasons.
When someone leaves,
I wish them well,
for I know a secret—
the sooner I let go,
joy will abound
with an amazing grace.
In every season,
I am always the heart
who beats behind the change.
Oh, beautiful soul
I excitedly await,
when you meet mine.
We will weather the seasons together.

# HIGHER LOVE

I choose you
because you elevate my spirit,
enrich my soul,
enhance my joy,
and encourage my love.
You bring out the best in me.
Falling for you was easy,
and staying in love with you
is even easier.

# FULL EXPRESSION

Our souls came to Earth
to express themselves—
body, mind, and spirit.
In this dimension,
I am excited to meet your soul
to fully engage in our wholeness
and experience the power of love
in this form,
time,
and space.

## GUIDED

How about we let our souls
find each other?
Letting it guide us where to go
and surrendering to what it knows.
Giving it full reign over our lives
while releasing the grip on the wheel.
As we let go,
allowing the force of magnetism
to connect our souls.

# MADE FROM SCRATCH

I didn't know someone like you
existed in the world.
I thought God would have to
make you from scratch for me—
I think he did.
I think maybe God did make you for me
because he made you perfect for me—
body, mind, spirit and soul.

# FIRE IN MY SOUL

I have this fire that burns inside me;
it has kept my soul alive.
I don't think I would have
made it this far,
if I didn't know you were out
there, too.
I have a passion for you,
a joy that lives inside me
that I'm ready to share with you.
I am waiting for you
to greet my soul.
I'm ready for fireworks,
how about you?

## MY STORYBOOK

I forgot about fairy tales
and princes and princesses.
I forgot about birthday wishes
and candles and dreams,
until you walked into my life
and then I fell into the most
extraordinary storybook
of my life.
You are my king.
I am your queen.
Us together,
blissfully joyous,
blissfully love,
our souls unite.

## OUR DESTINY

I'm going to let go of the idea
that I'm not ready,
or that you aren't ready.
Without those ideas,
nothing separates us.

# I WANT YOU

I don't want what everyone else has;
I want what we have—
belly laughs,
milk snorts,
jumping embraces,
soft kisses,
passionate kisses,
20-second kisses,
hand-holding everywhere,
best-friend cheers,
deep love,
witnessing God moments,
sharing everything.

# PERFECT GIFT

You were the most challenging relationship
I ever had
and back then,
I would have begged for it to change.
But now,
I wish nothing to be different—
my healing,
my forgiveness,
my heartbreak,
my return to love.
It all opened me
to the most beautiful love—
a love that builds me,
a love that cherishes me,
a love that grows me,
a love that holds me,
a love that adores me,
a love that loves beyond themselves,
this is the gift you left me.

# THANKFUL

We greet—
by honouring each other
responding in love,
listening to empathize,
respecting positions,
and seeing the truth.
But most importantly,
being grounded in gratitude,
that we found each other
to share this precious life.

# SOUL CONNECTION

Through the eyes of my soul,
I knew you were
the right one.
It was like God was congratulating
me for not giving up,
for surviving the lessons,
and for holding on to my faith.
My relationship with you
feels like an easy summer day,
a greased bike chain,
strolling through a meadow.
This is what I imagined
a love of wholeness to be.
Your spirit speaks to my soul,
and I get to ride on
the wings of love with you.
I'm faithing our connection—
trusting in this divine bond.

## ALL SOUL

Without my shell,
without my hair,
without my skin,
without my limbs,
without my face,
without all of this,
dear soul—
do you love me?

# FOUND

What a beautiful thing
to meet a soulmate—
someone that I don't
have to explain my soul to.
My soul has never felt so understood—
so at peace in your presence.
I haven't spoken these words to you;
It feels like our souls have already
communicated this each other.
I feel it deep inside me.
I get to express it in all ways possible—
body, mind, heart and soul
I feel found by you.
I would have never experienced this beauty
had I not risked loving myself
so passionately.

## PRESENTS

Everything that has ever happened
in my life
has led to this moment.
I have no regrets,
I have nothing I can't accept,
I have learned a lot,
I have been blessed,
I have been saved more times
than I can count.
God brought me here,
no doubt,
to see this beautiful moment
that could have only transpired
because of
every experience,
every heartache,
every landmine,
every challenge.
He built my heart,
He built my character,
He built my gratitude,
so through me
I can live this beautiful present moment
that was perfectly created for me.

# VORTEX

When I started to get excited
about my shadows
and exposing them to the light and truth,
everything that separated me from love
vanished before my eyes.
I could see from my wholeness.
This transformation healed my spirit
and allowed my heart to open fully.
In this space,
I created a vortex,
and your heart was called to mine.
This is the beauty of becoming
naked to my soul.

# HELLO

I don't want to play
hide-and-seek anymore.
Here I am.

# SOUL SET FREE

When I let go of all the expectations,
when I let go of all the programs,
when I let go of all the pressures,
is when I released the gifts of my life—
the natural beauty of who I am,
the natural beauty of my existence,
the natural beauty of my wholeness.
And with such ease
you flowed into my life,
you are my soul set free.

# FULLNESS

I love who I am in your presence—
fully woman,
fully loved,
fully myself.
This is what happened
when I fell in love with my wholeness.
This happened
when I accepted
that I deserved the best in my life.
Life mirrored truth back to me.

# BEING HELD

I love you—
the way you are polite with your actions,
the careful way you speak to my heart,
the kind way you touch my soul,
the tender way you comfort my wholeness,
the strength of your conviction.
I love your soul.

# UNITED

The harder my heart broke,
the more I learned how to love myself.
I collected all the tiny pieces
that carried the essence of love
and I built my heart back,
stronger and more loving.
When I finished,
my heart charged back
stronger than ever
and that's when you came,
to share the beauty of true love—
me, you and us.

# IN THE PLAN

I'm glad God took
some people out of my life,
no matter how much it hurt
at the time.
God worked with my soul,
to heal it,
to clean it,
to free it,
and to love it.
I wouldn't have believed
you were on the other side of all that—
there is a destiny for all of us.

# THE BEST PART

The first part of my life,
was all about the lessons,
hardships, and difficulties.
This next half is my life,
is all about enjoying,
loving, and playing.
You in?

# SOUL KNOWING

I knew you were my soulmate
when I met you
because we shared an energy
of happiness, easiness, and rawness.
I felt seen and heard—
an excitement of being known.
You saw me in my wholeness,
and I saw you in yours—
it was like there was no separation
even though we were in different bodies.
We cared for each other
in unspoken ways—
telling our souls what they needed to hear
and giving us everything
words could not.
Like magnets,
our souls found each other.

# WHEN GOD WINKS

There are no accidents or coincidences—
everything that has happened in life;
was meant to happen.
You were meant to come from your parents
and I was meant to come from mine.
You were meant to have your challenges
and gifts
and I was meant to have mine.
In a whirlwind,
we were making our way to each other.
Like attracts like.
Meeting you,
was less like a chance
and more like an inevitability—
God doesn't roll dice.

# DIFFERENT WAY

I tried so hard to find you.
It became a habit
of not finding you.
So I let go.
I would rather live this life
without you,
than live it with someone
that isn't you.
And so here I am.
I let go of trying.
I let go of this habit.
In my new approach,
I let it be easy.
I let it all be new.
My soul has a better way.

# YIN AND YANG

I had never met a man
who was so kind,
not only in front of my face
but everywhere he went.
He redefined what I considered
to be a masculine man,
leading people with confidence
and humility.
He could feel his emotions,
which made him trustworthy.
He could hold space and strength
to support those who needed to be held.
This yang foundation
is necessary
for the yin to dance.

# MATE TO MY SOUL

I have imagined your face,
but I can't see it.
I have imagined the colour of your hair,
but I can't see it.
I have imagined what you smell like,
but I can't smell it.
I have imagined what your voice sounds
like,
but I can't hear it.
I have imagined what your kiss feels like,
but I can't feel it.
I have imagined what your soul feels like
and this is undeniably recognizable—
because it feels like
my favourite memory,
mixed with my favourite moment,
and topped with my favourite vision.

# BOY BECOMES MAN

I appreciate the boy who has loved
everyone in his life.
I appreciate the boy who has forgiven
everything bad in his life.
I appreciate the boy who has desired
the girl of his dreams.
I appreciate the purity of the boy
who has walked a girl home with chivalry.
I appreciate the boy who knew
his heart was his treasure.
And now this boy has become a man;
I respect this man.
He takes care of the boy within himself,
he loves,
he forgives,
he believes in the woman of his dreams,
he respects the essence of beauty
in the everyday,
and he loves with his whole heart.
This is the man for me.

# MY TIME

This time,
it will be a hell yes.
This time,
I will follow my heart.
This time,
I will use my words
to be honest and authentic.
This time,
I will speak the truth.
This time,
I will be in integrity.
This time,
I am receiving what's mine.

## SOUL CALL

In this poem,
if I can be so bold—
if you are out there
would you let me know?
Please send me a sign that you will;
wait for me,
care for me,
be patient with me,
fight for me,
grow with me,
laugh with me,
cry with me,
hold me,
seek for me,
and never let me go.

# BRIGHT EYES

When I first saw you,
I felt you in my heart—
I can look into those eyes forever.
I never want to make those happy eyes—
sad.
My soul has been waiting for you
to appear in my life—
in this life.
Thank you for finding your way—
you are mine
and I am yours.

# RECEIVING MODE

We all love, love.
True love is the epitome
of our existence.
I'm not settling anymore.
I deserve love—
all I have been pouring out of me.
Can I receive this love that I am?
A love that is:
attentive,
kind,
fun,
truthful,
patient,
forgiving
and dedicated.
Instead of seeking
something mysterious—
this is the love
I am open to receiving.
This is the love I know
in my soul.

## MY STORY OF US

I'm writing a new story today.
This is my love story,
and how it unfolds.
God brings us together.
You are crazy handsome
and crazy nerdy.
You think I am crazy beautiful
and crazy nerdy.
We both want marriage,
we both want kids,
we know it happens quickly
when it's right.
We laugh and are comfortable
with each other—best friend energy.
We love, love.
We are content with ourselves
to give our all to this.
We want Heaven on Earth together
and we will create it.
This is the story of Us.

# ATTRACTION

What excites me the most
is that I get to experience all
these beautiful moments of life
with you.
You add to my life,
and that is why I feel blessed.
An attraction continues
to grow between us
because we are constantly growing.
You peel back your layers,
and I peel back mine.
You help me remember more
of who I am in your eyes.
And I do the same for you.
Our two whole parts
join to create a megaforce.
Being with you,
helps me to remember
that we are both charged batteries,
but together,
we are a powerhouse.

# NATURAL

It wasn't complicated.
Our energies attracted
us to each other.
We felt more excited and joyous
when close to each other.
We both shared the truth
that beat in our hearts.
We were both ready to give
to our union—
which made us mesh so well.
The way we met—
felt like destiny for both of us.
In being ourselves,
things moved quickly.
Inspired by instinct
and intuition—
it came together naturally.

# ENDS OF THE EARTH

With you,
I know you have the power
to crush my heart again.
I have put my heart
into every relationship
I have ever had.
I have been hurt more times
than I care to count.
I believe in love—
people caring about others
until the ends of the earth.
Wisdom has taught me
not everyone is capable of this.
I don't want to lose this part of me—
because I love this quality about me.
There aren't many people for me,
and I am now well aware.
I'm not putting energy where
it doesn't belong any more.
I'm letting my heart and soul,
reveal to me
whether you are fair-weathered
or will stand the tests of time.

heart-to-heart, soul-to-soul

# I NEED YOU

You make me feel again.
A part of me thought maybe
I would have to do this all alone.
My heart calls to yours.
God has shown me a lot of men.
It took me a long time to see
that easy men
don't do anything for me.
I like solid men
who put their heart
into everything they do.
I like the guys who still care
and will go the extra mile.
I like men who do quality work,
more than just enough to get by.
I like consistent men
who are intentional with their actions—
leaving no room for confusion.
I see it all the time.
And you are different.
I needed different.
I needed you.

# RIDE OR DIE

I have been through things
I thought I would die from.
I have been with people
who have brought hell to life.
It isn't easy to disregard
all these things.
But I do know—
I have experienced wonderful things
that have made me appreciate it all,
and I have met wonderful people
who have helped me experience heaven.
I know life comes with bad and good;
and everything can be transformed
to be made better.
Knowing this wisdom,
it only makes sense
for me to want to do it all
with my ride or die—
to face it all with me.

# DISCOVERY

In diving deep in my life,
I know my counterpart on Earth,
is another soul who has dove deep.
This is a superficial place,
where people hide themselves
to belong, to work, to exist.
I have met souls
who have appeared to be pretty
on the outside,
hiding such evil on the inside.
I have met souls
who have appeared to be nasty
on the outside,
hiding such love on the inside.
It is a process to discover the truth.
I believe that is why
it's taken me some time to find you—
the soul who has done the work
to refine their character
while maintaining the beauty
of their soul—
pretty and lovely to their core.

## OUR HOME

We are a balance to each other.
I accept you as you are.
You accept me as I am.
I can be more myself
around you because I am free
to be adored and safe.
You can be more yourself
around me because you are free
to be admired and appreciated.
This is why it works.
This is why we fit.
This is why we are home
to each other.

## ART

My relationship with you
is indefinable—
which is precisely why it is beautiful.
It is like all the colours
that exist in the world,
at this moment,
at that moment,
and any variation in-between.
It allows us to paint any picture
we like,
whenever we like,
however we like.
It is possibility upon possibility.
Thank you for creating art with me.

## SURREAL LOVE

I will trust in the truth
that lives in my soul.
It tells me I have a soul partner
who is seeking me, too.
We both desire a surreal love,
not one that is born
in a world like this,
but is heaven sent.
I have tried worldly love,
and it doesn't fulfill my soul.
It leaves me hopeless and fragmented.
I am ready for a soul love
that is high-spirited and whole.

## APPLE SHOPPING

After a few bad apples,
you might think
there are no good apples.
Finding love can often feel
like apple-picking.
You have to remind yourself
that finding your person
is more like a shopping process;
sometimes there is a lousy shipment,
sometimes it's a bad season,
sometimes there is global chaos,
sometimes there is an inventory shortage,
sometimes there is access denial,
sometimes there are quality control issues.
Some things are
out of your control,
so enjoy whatever is happening
and stay inspired.
You will be ready for the—
the best apples to come when
you stay expectant for it.
There will always be a delicious one
ripe for you
if you are patient.

sakura hanami

# HEART OF MY SOUL

My soul is forever,
so that is the kind of love I seek.
I don't want the temporary highs,
and the constant pains of this world.
I want to share a love
that doesn't make me question
what love means,
or its ability to sustain itself.
I am here to let go
with another soul—
who speaks the language
of the heart of my soul.

heart-to-heart, soul-to-soul

# YOUR SUPPORT

In meeting you,
you have taught me,
I needed someone like you
to show me I could be loved for;
the developed and developing
parts of me—
my vulnerability when I am not
feeling my best,
my softness when I let go of control,
my courage when I allow myself
to be seen,
my willingness to share who I am,
and the support to be everything
I have ever dreamed.

## EMPOWERED

When our souls met,
everything was simple.
I felt at ease in your company
and all fears were dashed away.
I had a partner who would be
equally committed and loyal
to our journey to experience deeper love.
I knew you were my match
because for the first time,
I met someone who could unselfishly
give two hundred percent
from a pure heart.
I have done as much as I could
to empower myself throughout my life,
and with our energies combined,
I feel a power that effortlessly spins
our world with a beautiful life of its own.

## OUR EXPRESSION

I feel blessed
we both have committed
to do this life with each other.
Thank you for loving, trusting
and honouring me
while I express
my individuality and uniqueness.
With you,
I can live more,
share more,
feel more,
and love more.
Thank you for our connection
and our special love
that enhances my existence.

# TRUTH

Our journey is to express truth—
the truth of who we are,
the truth of love,
the truth of letting ourselves be free.
Thank you for sharing
your journey with me
and allowing me to see more
of all these truths.
In my heart,
together,
we can help show each other
how to trust more,
love more,
and express more.
What a beautiful gift this is.

# LOVE IS FREEDOM

Love isn't scary—
it's the experiences
we associated with it,
that caused us to believe mistakenly
that love is painful.
Everything that isn't true love
is what is painful.
Love itself is freedom—
joy-filled,
fun,
enduring,
accepting,
honoring,
supportive.
Love is everything
that makes us feel alive
and keeps us growing.

# WELCOME

I allow you to accept me—
the parts I perceive
to be good, bad, and everything
in-between.
Thank you for creating a safe space
free of judgements
and supporting me to free myself
as I uncover and reveal
more of who I am.
As my mirror,
I welcome all of who you are.

We all have a special person who perfectly complements our souls. If you need a sign they exist, this is it. I pray for you as you call in the one, my friend.

And if you have found each other, I pray you continue to grow in love.

Thank you for purchasing my book.

I would love it if you could review my book to share what
you enjoyed with others. I pray the words in this book
will let your heart overflow with love to share. Thank you.
I sincerely appreciate it.

Sign up for my newsletter: sakura-hanami.com
TIKTOK: @love.sakura.hanami
Twitter: @sakura_h_writes

www.ingramcontent.com/pod-product-compliance
Lightning Source LLC
Chambersburg PA
CBHW031339060726
47590CB00007B/2548